KU-235-513

Wartime Cookbook

Food and Recipes from the Second World War 1939–45

Alison Cooper

HODDER
Wayland

an imprint of Hodder Children's Books

Titles in this Series:
The Home Front
Wartime Cookbook

For more information on this series and other Hodder Wayland titles, go to
www.hodderwayland.co.uk

Picture acknowledgements
The publisher would like to thank the following for allowing their pictures to be reproduced
in this book: Corbis cover background; Getty cover main; Hulton Deutsch 38 bottom;
Imperial War Museum title page, 6 bottom, 7, 8, 9 top, 10, 11 both, 12 both, 13, 14 both,
15, 16, 18, 20, 21, 22, 28, 29, 30, 32 both, 33, 39, 40, 43, 45; Peter Newark's Historical
Pictures 5, 9 bottom, 25, 26 both, 36 top; Popperfoto 24, 42; Topham Picture Library 4
both, 6 top, 17, 19, 23 both, 34, 35, 36 bottom, 37, 38 top, 41, 44 both. The artwork was
supplied by Jenny Hughes.

Cover: a young girl with her food rations.
Title page: a Guernsey family enjoying a victory meal.

This book is based on the original title *Wartime Cookbook* by Anne and Brian Moses.
First published in Great Britain in 1995 by Wayland (Publishers) Ltd

This differentiated text version by Alison Cooper, published in 2005 by Hodder Wayland, an
imprint of Hodder Children's Books

© Hodder Wayland 2005

Hodder Children's Books, a division of Hodder Headline Limited, 338 Euston Road,
London NW1 3BH

All rights reserved. Apart from any use permitted under UK copyright law, this publication
may only be reproduced, stored or transmitted, in any form, or by any means with prior
permission in writing of the publishers or in the case of reprographic production in
accordance with the terms of licences issued by the Copyright Licensing Agency.

Original designer: Malcolm Walker
Layout for this edition: Simon Borrough
Editor for this edition: Hayley Leach

British Library Cataloguing in Publication Data
Cooper, Alison, 1967-
        Wartime cookbook
        1.World War, 1939-1945 – Food supply – Greta Britain –
Juvenile literature 2.Rationing – Great Britain – History –
20th century – Juvenile literature 3.World War, 1939-1945 –
Social aspects – Great Britain – Juvenile literature
        4.Great Britain – Social conditions – 20th century
Juvenile literature
        I.Title
        941'.084

ISBN: 0750247592

Printed in China by WKT Company Ltd

STAFFORDSHIRE LIBRARIES
ARTS AND ARCHIVES

38014040022904	
PET	27-Oct-05
C941.08	£12.99
KINV	

Contents

Words that appear in **bold** can be found in the glossary on page 46.

The Battle for Food Begins

The Second World War began on 3 September 1939, when Britain and France declared war on Germany. The fighting lasted for nearly six years. Many more countries became involved.

British people had to face many changes to their everyday lives when war broke out. One of these changes was **rationing**.

Above Germany's invasion of Poland led to Britain entering the war.

Above Supplies being unloaded from ships at a busy British **dockyard**.

Before the war, two thirds of Britain's food was **imported** by ship. Once the war began, German **U-boats** started to sink ships carrying these vital supplies.

The government was worried that wealthy people would buy all the imported supplies that were available. This would mean that poorer people could not buy foods such as tea or sugar. Rationing was a way of making sure that everyone got a fair share of the food that was available.

Above Many sailors died when supply ships were sunk or damaged. This poster thanks them for their bravery.

APPLE JELLY

Ask an adult to help you peel and slice ½ lb (225 g) of apples. Put the apples into a saucepan, cover with water and cook gently until tender. Sweeten with 1 dessertspoon of honey and flavour with cinnamon or ginger. Whip the mixture until light and frothy. Dissolve ½ tablet of jelly in ¼ pint (125 ml) hot water. Leave to cool, then stir in the apple mixture. Leave to set overnight in the fridge.

How Rationing Worked

A new government department was set up to organize **rationing**. It was called the Ministry of Food.

Everybody in the country – even the royal family – was given a ration book. They had to register at the grocer's and butcher's shops where they wanted to buy their rationed food. People who travelled around a lot, such as lorry drivers, had a special kind of ration book because they could not buy their rations in the same place every week.

Above People still had to pay for their food but they had to have a ration book like the ones in this picture as well.

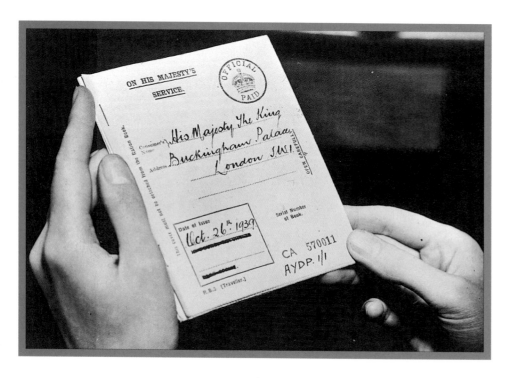

Left This ration book belonged to King George VI.

LORD WOOLTON'S VEGETABLE PIE

This recipe was named after Lord Woolton because he was the Minister for Food.

2 lb (1 kg) potatoes
1 lb (450 g) cauliflower
1 lb (450 g) carrots
½ lb (225 g) swede
½ lb (225 g) parsnips
3 or 4 spring onions
water for cooking
1 teaspoon (5 ml) vegetable extract
1 tablespoon (15 ml) oatmeal
chopped parsley
2 oz (50 g) grated cheese

With an adult's help, cook half the potatoes, the vegetables, the vegetable extract and oatmeal for 10 minutes in enough water to cover them. Stir occasionally to prevent sticking. Cool and place in a pie dish. Sprinkle with chopped parsley. Boil the rest of the potatoes and mash them. Spread them over the vegetables and sprinkle the cheese on top. Bake at 190ºC, gas mark 5, until lightly browned. Serve with gravy and vegetables. Serves 6–8.

Below The shopkeeper is stamping the book to show that the customer has bought their ration.

Rationing began on 8 January 1940. At first, only butter, sugar, ham and bacon were rationed. When people wanted to buy these foods, they handed their ration book to the shopkeeper. Once the shopkeeper had stamped their book, they could not buy more rations until the following week.

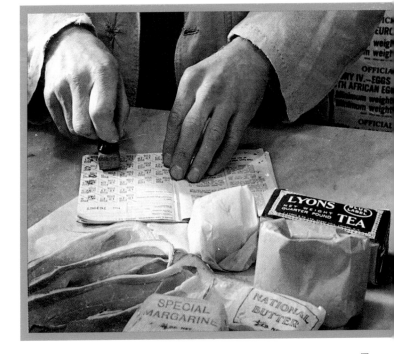

More Rationing

More foods were rationed during 1940 – meat, tea, cooking fats and margarine. The sugar ration was cut from 12 oz (350 g) per person per week, to 8 oz (225 g) per person per week.

In the morning we used to get up and my Mum always used to be making porridge. But because sugar was on ration it tasted horrible...
Then I remember Mum found a tin of syrup in the cupboard and instead of having sugar on porridge we had syrup and it was delicious.

Children of the Blitz *by Robert Westall*

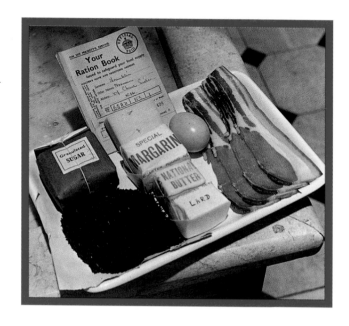

Above This photograph shows the typical amount of rationed food that an adult was allowed each week.

MACARONI AND BACON DISH

½ oz (12.5 g) **dripping,** or other fat
2 oz (50 g) leek or onion, peeled and chopped
2 oz (50 g) bacon, chopped
1 pint (500 ml) vegetable stock, made by dissolving a
    vegetable stock cube in boiling water
6 oz (150 g) macaroni
salt and pepper

With an adult's help, melt the dripping in a pan and fry the leek and bacon until lightly browned. Add the stock, bring to the boil, and add the macaroni, salt and pepper. Cook for 20 minutes or until the macaroni is tender. Garnish with watercress. Serves 4.

Above Displays like these showed people how to make the best use of the food they had.

In 1941, a new way of sharing out food began. Each person was allowed 16 points every month, as well as their rations. They could use their points to buy foods such as dried fruit, biscuits and tinned meat or fish. Each of these foods was worth a certain number of points. So, for example, if someone wanted to make a fruit cake, they would need to use all their 16 points to buy 2 lb (1 kg) of dried fruit.

Right This newspaper article explains how to cook salt fish.

Dig for Victory

The government knew that it was important to grow more food in Britain, as well as **rationing** food that was **imported**. The Ministry of Food began a 'Dig for Victory' **campaign**. Posters encouraged people to use every spare bit of land to grow vegetables.

The campaign was a great success. People dug up their lawns and planted vegetables instead. Potatoes and carrots grew in parks and on railway embankments. Marrows sprouted from the soil that was piled on top of **air-raid shelters.**

Below Even the dried-up moat at the Tower of London was turned into a vegetable garden.

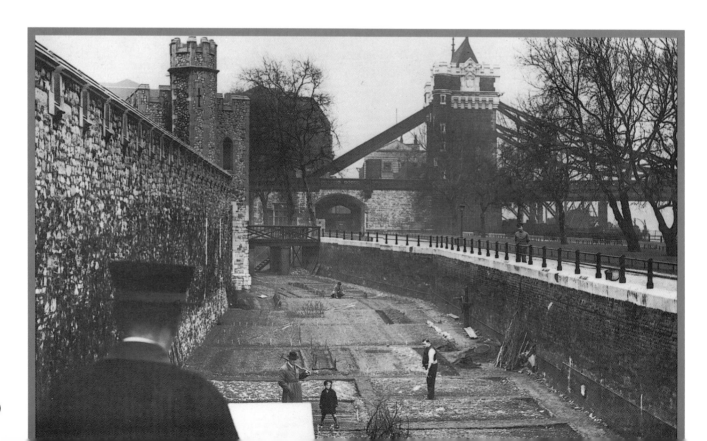

MARROW PUDDING

With an adult's help, boil a small marrow in water and drain it in a colander. Fill a pie dish three quarters full with the marrow. Add a lump of butter and a little sugar and spice for flavouring. Fill up the dish with milk. Bake it on an oven tray for 45 minutes at 190ºC, gas mark 5. Serves 4.

Above Huge posters like this made it impossible to ignore the 'Dig for Victory' campaign.

Below This woman is watering the vegetables growing on top of her air-raid shelter.

*Dig! Dig! Dig! And your
    muscles will grow big,
Keep on pushing the spade!
Don't mind the worms,
Just ignore their squirms,
And when your back aches
    laugh with glee
And keep on diggin'
Till we give our foes a wiggin'
Dig! Dig! Dig! to victory.*
                    Wartime song

Wartime Farming

Above Land girls using a potato planter.

Right A poster asking women to work on farms.

Britain's farms needed to produce more food than ever but many men had left their farm jobs and joined the **armed forces.** The government wanted women to take over the work on farms so it set up the Women's Land Army.

Women in the Land Army were known as 'Land Girls'. They milked cows, planted crops and harvested them.

Come and help with the

VICTORY HARVEST

You are needed in the fields!

APPLY TO NEAREST EMPLOYMENT EXCHANGE FOR LEAFLET & ENROLMENT FORM
OR WRITE DIRECT TO THE DEPARTMENT OF AGRICULTURE FOR SCOTLAND
15 GROSVENOR STREET, EDINBURGH.

lend a hand on the land

at a farming holiday camp

Left Children helped on farms during the school holidays.

New machines were invented, such as the potato planter shown on page 12. These helped farmers to do their jobs more quickly and meant they could produce a lot more crops.

PARSNIP PUDDING

Mash 2 medium-sized cooked cold parsnips with a tablespoon of cocoa. Add a pinch of bicarbonate of soda. With an adult's help, warm ½ pint (250 ml) of milk and sweeten with sugar. Add the milk to the parsnip mixture and mix together. Bake for 30 minutes at 190ºC, gas mark 5. Serves 4.

Doctor Carrot

Left Doctor Carrot was a cartoon character invented by the Ministry of Food.

DOCTOR CARROT the Children's best friend

VIT-A

Below It was hard to get raw fruit during the war, so people had to eat more green vegetables to stay healthy.

Carrots contain vitamin A, which is important for good eyesight. The cartoon character Dr Carrot suggested people would be able to see better in the **blackout** if they ate lots of carrots. This was not really true because it would take a lot of carrots to improve people's eyesight in the dark! Dr Carrot suggested new recipes using carrots but not everyone enjoyed them.

GREEN VEGETABLES & SALADS
help you to resist infection, clear the skin, and take the place of raw fruit.

CARROT COOKIES

1 tablespoon (15 ml) margarine
2 tablespoons (30 ml) sugar
a few drops of vanilla, almond or orange flavouring
4 tablespoons (60 ml) grated raw carrot
6 tablespoons (90 ml) self-raising flour, or plain flour and
½ teaspoon (2.5 ml) baking powder
extra sugar to sprinkle on top of the cookies

Mix the margarine and sugar together until light and fluffy.
Beat in the flavouring and grated carrot. Gently stir in the flour, or
plain flour and baking powder. Drop spoonfuls of the mixture into
small greased patty pans. Sprinkle the tops with the extra sugar
and bake at 220°C, gas mark 7, for about 20 minutes. Makes 12
to 15 cookies.

One morning a jar was put on the breakfast table . . . My father spread the nectar on his bread and bit into it. He frowned and said: 'What was that?' 'Carrot marmalade,' said my mother. . . .he picked up the jar . . . and poured it on the compost heap.

The Sheltered Days *by Derek Lambert*

Left This restaurant is advertising 'Victory' meals. These were made from vegetables and other foods that did not have to be **imported.**

Potato Pete

As well as inventing Dr Carrot, the Ministry of Food created a cartoon character called Potato Pete. They used him in adverts to encourage people to eat more potatoes. There was even a song about him:

Potato Pete, Potato Pete,
See him coming down the street,
Shouting his good things to eat,
'Get your hot potatoes
From Potato Pete.'

All sorts of new recipes were invented. They explained how to use potatoes in pastry, puddings, sandwiches and even cakes.

Left Potato Pete was a jolly cartoon character.

Left These schoolboys are hard at work, digging up potatoes as part of their school lessons.

The Ministry of Food wanted people to fill up on potatoes instead of eating bread. Most of the wheat used to make bread had to be **imported** but potatoes could easily be grown in Britain. Potatoes also contain vitamin C, which is important because it helps people to stay healthy.

POTATO PIGLETS

People could use this recipe instead of making sausage rolls. But even sausages were hard to get during the war.

6 medium potatoes, well scrubbed
6 skinned sausages

Use an apple corer to make a hole through each potato. Stuff each hole with a sausage. Bake the potatoes for about an hour at 220°C, gas mark 7. Serve on a pile of chopped cabbage – cooked or raw.

Ask an adult to make the holes in the potatoes for you.

Keeping Animals

Some people kept animals to use for food. 'Pig clubs' were popular. Several families or a group of workers would all help to feed a pig. When it was time for the pig to be killed, everyone got a share of the meat.

Left London policemen cleaning out a pig sty.

This is a report about a pig club run by some policemen in London.

The sty that houses these important pigs was. . .built like a gaol. Evidently the police were afraid the pigs might escape.

Farmers' Weekly, 1941

LIVER SAVOURY

You can use any kind of liver in this recipe. Chop ¼ lb (100 g) liver into small pieces, coat them in flour and fry in **dripping.** Cover 4 slices of stale bread with sliced tomatoes, sprinkle with cheese, dot with small lumps of fat, and grill quickly. Place the fried liver on the grilled bread and serve.

Ask an adult to help you chop and fry the liver and use the grill.

People kept chickens mainly for their eggs. It was easy to keep a few chickens in the garden. Some people even managed to keep them on flat roofs or balconies in the middle of towns! Chickens that did not produce many eggs could be killed and eaten.

Rabbits were kept in the garden. The Ministry of Food encouraged people to eat rabbit meat.

Below This couple have a small chicken coop in their garden.

Saving the Scraps

Supply ships crossed the Atlantic Ocean from North America to Britain in groups called convoys. Warships sailed with them for protection. But the **U-boats** became more and more successful at sinking the ships. The struggle against the U-boats was called the Battle of the Atlantic.

In Britain, rations became smaller, because so few supplies were able to reach the country. People could be fined for wasting bread. A few people still did not understand how serious the shortages were, as this newspaper report shows.

The servant was twice seen throwing bread to the birds in the garden, and when Miss O'Sullivan was interviewed she admitted that bread was put out every day. 'I cannot see the birds starve,' she said.

Bristol Evening Post,
20 January 1943

Below This woman has a chart on her kitchen wall that shows how much meat, cheese, potatoes and other food people needed for a healthy diet.

CHEESE PUDDING

½ pint (250 ml) milk
2 eggs
4 oz (100 g) grated cheese
1 cup breadcrumbs
salt and pepper
¼ teaspoon (1 ml) dried mustard

Mix the milk and eggs together, then stir in the other ingredients. With an adult's help, bake in a greased ovenproof dish at 200ºC, gas mark 6, for about 30 minutes, until brown and set. Serves 4.

Below Even small children helped to fill the pig bins.

Thoughtful people put their kitchen scraps into pig bins. These were collected and the waste food was made into **pig swill**. The Ministry of Food reminded everyone:

*Because of the scraps,
  the pigs were saved,
Because of the pigs,
  the rations were saved,
Because of the rations,
  the ships were saved,
Because of the ships, the
  island [Britain] was saved.*

Saving Fuel

Coal was a very important fuel. It was burned in power stations to produce electricity. Most people used coal to heat their homes. Even gas was made by burning coal.

The factories that produced weapons and military equipment needed a lot of fuel to power their machines. People had to use as little fuel at home as possible.

Left Leaving food on the plate was not just a waste of food – it was also a waste of the fuel used to cook it. This poster reminds people to eat up everything.

Left This woman has filled a bag with coal and is using a pram to carry it home.

The Ministry of Power and Fuel gave people advice about saving fuel:

Never heat the oven for one cake or pudding, plan a baking day. Arrange with neighbours to share ovens, a cake might be baked while a casserole is slowly cooking or two joints of meat could be cooking at the same time.

Above This boy is collecting wood from bombed houses. People could save coal by burning wood on their fires at home.

SKIRLY-MIRLY

With an adult's help, boil equal amounts of peeled potatoes and peeled swedes in separate pans until tender. Drain well. Mash the potatoes and swedes into a smooth paste and mix well. Add a little hot milk and margarine. Season with pepper. Serve piled in a hot vegetable dish.

Strange Foods

Above These men have been out shooting wild rabbits for extra meat to eat.

Everyday foods were used in unusual ways during the Second World War – carrot marmalade, for example. People also had to try foods that were completely new to them, such as dried eggs.

Packets of dried egg were much easier to transport than fresh eggs, and the dried eggs were sent from the USA. From 1942, everyone was allowed one packet of dried egg each month. The Ministry of Food produced leaflets to explain that dried eggs were just as good for people as fresh eggs. Only the shells and the water had been removed.

People also searched the countryside for eggs from wild birds. One woman remembered collecting gulls' eggs.

We got a big bucketful each, and they were as big as ducks' eggs . . . It was absolutely legal then but you wouldn't be allowed to take the eggs today.

The Wartime Kitchen and Garden
by Jennifer Davis

Some people caught wild birds to eat – a restaurant in London once had roasted eagle on its menu.

NO EGG SHORTAGE
—a dozen a month for everybody!

SOME TIPS ON MAKING DELICIOUS EGG DISHES

"Take a dozen eggs," said Mrs. Beeton. Well, the present allowance of dried eggs means a dozen eggs a *week* for the average family, more than most people used before the war!

Remember that dried eggs are new-laid shell eggs with only the shell and the water taken away.

Make an omelette by allowing 3 or 4 eggs for two people. "Reconstitute" the eggs, add seasoning, beat well, and cook in smoking hot fat until all the egg is set. Cook it *quickly*, and don't overcook.

When making cakes and puddings, add the eggs *dry* to the other ingredients and add the water afterwards. Eggs are a grand nourishing food for children and dried eggs have the full nutritional value of shell eggs.

Don't mix dried eggs with water until you are ready to use them.

A packet of 12 Dried Eggs costs only 1/3

Issued by the Ministry of Food, London, W.1

Above This advertisement from the Ministry of Food explains how to use dried eggs.

EGGLESS SPONGE

6 oz (150 g) self-raising flour
1 teaspoon (5 ml) baking powder
2 ½ oz (65 g) margarine
2 oz (50 g) sugar
1 tablespoon (15 ml) golden syrup
¼ pint (125 ml) milk or milk and water
jam for filling

Sift the flour and baking powder. Mix the margarine, sugar and golden syrup until light and soft. Add a little flour and then a little milk or milk and water and mix it in. Continue adding the flour and liquid like this until the mixture is smooth. Grease two 18 cm cake tins and sprinkle them lightly with flour. Divide the mixture between them and bake at 200°C, gas mark 6, for about 20 minutes or until firm to the touch. Tip out of the tins carefully and spread one cake with jam. Cover with the other cake.

Different Tastes

In 1941, Britain began to **import** tins of corned beef and Spam from the USA. These meats were quite popular and people thought up lots of ways to use them in their meals. Towards the end of the war, whale meat went on sale but many people did not like its oily taste. They were not keen on tinned snoek, a type of fish from the West Indies, either.

Toothsome twosome...

SPAM 'N' SALAD

SPAM 'N' SALAD
Let cold sliced Spam join hands with your favorite salad. Ready in a jiffy for special company treat or family standby. (Spam is pure pork – rich in B₁ and B₂.)

HORMEL
GOOD FOODS

COLD OR HOT... **SPAM** HITS THE SPOT!

*"Spam" is a registered trademark. It identifies a meat product—packed only in 12-ounce tins—made exclusively by Geo. A. Hormel & Co., Austin, Minn.

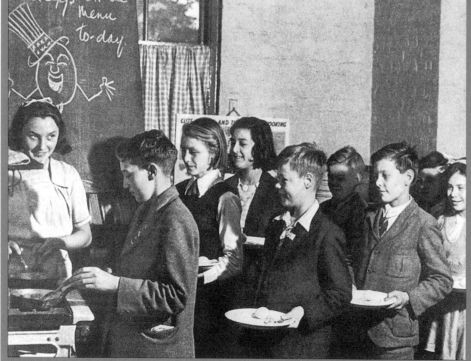

Above An advertisement for Spam, which was a mixture of pork meat and grains of cereal.

Left These schoolchildren are looking forward to a meal of bacon and eggs. The bacon had been imported from the USA.

CORNED BEEF HASH

8 oz (225 g) corned beef
8 oz (225 g) cooked potatoes
8 oz (225 g) tomatoes
½ oz (15 g) **dripping**
2 medium-sized onions, peeled and grated
salt and pepper

Cut the corned beef and potatoes into small cubes. Slice the tomatoes. Melt the dripping in a frying pan, add the onions and fry them gently until soft. Add the corned beef and potatoes. Cook for several minutes, then add the tomatoes, salt and pepper. Cover the pan with a lid and cook very gently for 15 minutes. Serves 4.

Ask an adult to help you with the chopping and frying.

The Channel Islands were occupied by the Germans in 1940. It became very difficult for the islanders to get enough food as the war went on. They made tea from dried **bramble** leaves or dried, grated carrots. They made a kind of 'coffee' from acorns, parsnips, wheat, sugar beet or lupin seeds. They even mixed dried seaweed with milk to make a kind of **blancmange**.

Right These women are packing whale meat into tins.

Fruits of the Countryside

One way to boost the rations was to gather wild food from fields, woods and hedgerows. The autumn was the best time for this. People searched for nuts, blackberries, mushrooms, crab apples and rosehips.

Every autumn weekend, groups from school fanned out over North Devon, . . . we picked for hours, our backs breaking in the search for the tiny bilberries hidden at ground level, and which the school cook made into jam.

Talking about the War
by Anne Valery

Below Groups of people cycled from the towns into the countryside to find nuts and berries.

Even dandelion leaves and stinging nettles could be put to good use:

*A poached egg on a bed of dandelion or nettle **purée** covered with cheese sauce is an almost perfect meal.* Kitchen Front Recipes and Hints *by Ambrose Heath*

Below These women are making jam from wild berries.

NETTLE TEA
Put on an old pair of gloves and pick some young stinging nettles. Wash the nettles and dry them in the sun. When dry, crumble up and boil in water to bring out the flavour. Nettle tea once a day makes a good, healthy drink.

Evacuees

Children were **evacuated** from towns and cities that were likely to be bombed, to safer areas. Some **evacuees** came from very poor families. They found many things about their new homes strange, including the food. Some were given porridge but wanted their usual breakfast of bread and lard. Many were not sure how to use a knife and fork. At home, they only had meals they could eat with their fingers.

Above These evacuees are having a meal at school.

TOAD IN THE HOLE

4 oz (100 g) plain flour
pinch of salt
1 egg or 1 tablespoon (15 ml) dried egg
½ pint (250 ml) milk (or milk and water mixed)
½ oz (15 g) lard
10–12 thin pork sausages

Beat the egg into the flour and salt and then gradually mix in the milk to make a batter. Put the sausages in a greased tin about 25 cm by 30 cm and cook for 5 or 10 minutes at 230°C, gas mark 7. When the fat starts to run out of the sausages, pour in the batter. Bake for 35 minutes until the batter is risen and well browned. Serves 4.

Ask an adult to help you use the oven.

Left Evacuees from the poorest city homes were not used to sitting at the table for a meal like this.

Not all the evacuees were unhappy. Many were eating the best food they had ever had in their lives. This boy, who was evacuated from London, was delighted with his new surroundings:

We never had breakfast in Stepney Green, just a cup of tea and a slice of bread. There we were, [with] a table all set out with knives and forks and marmalade. And we were eating soft-boiled eggs. Well, if this was evacuation, I was all for it.

The World is a Wedding
by Bernard Kops

MILK THE BACKBONE OF YOUNG BRITAIN

Above This poster reminds people that children need milk to develop strong bones. Some evacuees had rarely drunk milk before the war.

A Healthy Diet

Before the Second World War, there had been several years when it was hard for people to get work. Many people could hardly afford enough food for their families. Almost half the population of Britain was suffering from **malnutrition** when the war began. The government knew that if people were not well fed they would not have the strength or energy to fight battles or work long hours in farms and factories.

mother

don't forget baby's

COD LIVER OIL
AND ORANGE JUICE

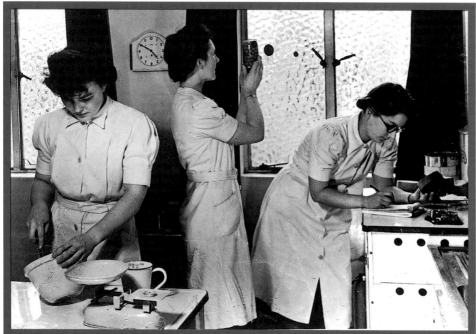

Above The health of babies improved because their mothers could get free **cod-liver oil** and orange juice for them.

Left Staff at the Ministry of Food worked out what types of food and how much food people needed to stay healthy.

QUICK VEGETABLE SOUP

½ oz (15 g) **dripping**
12 oz (350 g) mixed vegetables,
  chopped into cubes
1½ pints (750 ml) water or stock
salt and pepper
chopped parsley

With an adult's help, melt the dripping in a saucepan. Add the vegetables and cook gently for at least 5 minutes. Add the water or stock and cook gently for 25 minutes. Add salt and pepper, then push the mixture through a sieve to make a **purée**. Reheat and serve sprinkled with chopped parsley. Serves 4.

People often complained about **rationing,** but their wartime diet was actually better for their health.

Before the war we ate what was nice – fish and chips, sausages, pies, cakes, sweets – with hardly a green vegetable in sight.

Children of the Blitz *by Robert Westall*

Fatty and sugary foods like the sausages and sweets mentioned above were rationed. People had to fill up on fruit and vegetables instead.

From 1941, children under 2 years old were given blackcurrant or orange juice and cod-liver oil, which are rich in vitamins. Pregnant women and poor children were given free milk.

Below Fruit and vegetables were not rationed, so people bought more of them than they had done before the war.

The Wheatmeal Loaf

Pat-a-loaf, pat-a-loaf
Baker's Man
Bake me some Wheatmeal
As fast as you can:
It builds up my health
And its taste is so good,
I find that I like
Eating just what I should.

Wartime rhyme

This wartime version of a
nursery rhyme is about the
National Wheatmeal Loaf.
This was a loaf that was made
from the whole grain of the
wheat, instead of just the
inner part. It was much healthier than the white bread
that was usually eaten. Using all the grain meant that less
wheat had to be **imported,** too. But although the rhyme
says 'it tasted so good', people in Britain did not agree.
They thought it was 'nasty, dirty, coarse [and] dark'.

In the Channel Islands, which were occupied by the
Germans, bread was even worse. The islanders
sometimes found bits of straw, string or even
matchsticks in their loaves.

Don't ask for bread unless you really want it

JOIN THE CRUSADE AGAINST WASTE OF BREAD

Above This poster reminds people not to waste bread.

Ask an adult to help you with hot pans and the grill.

WELSH RAREBIT (USING STALE CRUSTS)

1½ oz (40 g) stale crusts, soaked in water and squeezed
4 tablespoons (60 ml) milk
2 oz (50 g) grated cheese
1 teaspoon (5 ml) mustard
1–2 teaspoons (5–10 ml) salt
pinch of pepper
½ oz (15 g) margarine
4 slices of toast

Mix the soaked bread with the milk, half the cheese and the salt and pepper. Beat well. Melt the margarine in a saucepan, then add the bread and cheese mixture and cook until hot and well blended. Spread it on the slices of toast and sprinkle with the remainder of the cheese. Brown gently under the grill. Serve very hot. Serves 4.

Below You can see the poster from page 34 on the wall of the restaurant in this photograph.

The Black Market

As the war went on, it became harder to make the rations last the week and meals were very boring. Some people were prepared to buy extra supplies of rationed food if they could get them. When someone had extra food to sell people would pass on the news to their friends and neighbours.

You'd probably hear that there'd be some sugar about somewhere, if you could find your way to it, which had 'fallen' off the back of a lorry.
The Wartime Kitchen and Garden *by Jennifer Davies*

Buying and selling goods like this was called the black market. Often, the goods were stolen from warehouses or from lorries taking food to the shops.

Right This man is putting up the **blackout** curtains in his café. It was easy for thieves to move through the dark streets during the blackout and take food from warehouses.

Above Feeding a family was a struggle.

Dock workers, rail workers, lorry drivers and shopkeepers were all involved in the black market. Lorry drivers, for example, might sign records to show that they had taken a certain amount of food and then take a bit extra. They would sell the extra food on to a shopkeeper.

People who were involved in the black market could be fined or imprisoned for up to two years, but some were prepared to take the risk.

Above This dock worker is unloading boxes of eggs from Australia. Records were kept of the goods that arrived but it was possible for some to 'disappear'.

CRUNCHIES

4 oz (100 g) margarine, lard or **dripping**
2 oz (50 g) sugar
2 oz (50 g) syrup
5 oz (125 g) plain flour
4 oz (100g) medium oatmeal
1 teaspoon (5 ml) baking powder
vanilla flavouring

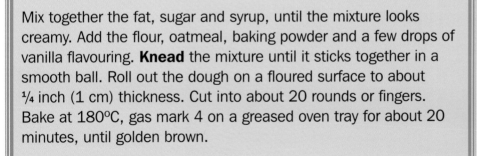

Mix together the fat, sugar and syrup, until the mixture looks creamy. Add the flour, oatmeal, baking powder and a few drops of vanilla flavouring. **Knead** the mixture until it sticks together in a smooth ball. Roll out the dough on a floured surface to about ¼ inch (1 cm) thickness. Cut into about 20 rounds or fingers. Bake at 180°C, gas mark 4 on a greased oven tray for about 20 minutes, until golden brown.

Sweet Treats

Sweets became a special treat. The amount people were allowed to buy was quite small – about the same weight as a medium-sized bar of chocolate, every four weeks. Adults often gave their sweet ration to children. American soldiers based in Britain sometimes gave children extra sweets and chewing gum.

Very little fruit was **imported** to Britain. Some young children had never seen bananas or oranges, and had no idea how to eat them.

Above This girl is deciding what sweets to get with her sweet ration.

Left An American soldier giving out sweets to British children.

UNCOOKED CHOCOLATE CAKE

2 oz (50 g) margarine
2 oz (50 g) sugar
2 tablespoons (30 ml) golden syrup
2 oz (50 g) cocoa powder
vanilla essence
6 oz (150 g) crisp breadcrumbs

Put the margarine, sugar and syrup into a saucepan. Ask an adult to help you heat the pan gently until the margarine has melted. Take the pan off the heat. Stir in the cocoa powder, a few drops of vanilla essence and the breadcrumbs. Mix everything together well. Grease an 18cm cake tin then pour in the mixture. Leave it for 4 or 5 hours, then turn it out carefully. Top with glossy chocolate icing.

To make crisp breadcrumbs, bake some pieces of bread in the oven until crispy (do this when something else is being baked, to save fuel). Leave them to cool, then crush them between two sheets of greaseproof paper with a rolling pin.

THE ICING

Mix together 2 teaspoons (10 ml) melted margarine, 1 tablespoon (15 ml) cocoa powder, 1 tablespoon (15 ml) golden syrup and a few drops of vanilla essence.

Where I lived there was a prisoner-of-war camp behind us. One day… a prisoner called us to the fence and offered us three bananas… Not knowing how to eat it we peeled the banana, ate the skin and threw the inner away.

Children of the Blitz
by Robert Westall

Below By the end of the war, people could hardly ever buy fruit that did not grow in Britain.

Eating Out

Left People who had lost their homes in the bombing could get a hot meal at a British restaurant.

People could avoid using their precious rations by eating at a restaurant because restaurant meals were not rationed. In the early part of the war, people could enjoy restaurant meals that had five or six courses, as long as they could afford to pay for them. This seemed very unfair when most people were only getting their basic rations. By 1942, the Ministry of Food had limited restaurant meals to one basic main dish.

From 1940, people whose homes had been bombed could get a cheap meal in a restaurant set up by the government. These were called 'British restaurants'. By 1943, there were over 2,000 British restaurants and they served 600,000 meals a day.

Before the war people were used to being served at their table by a waiter or waitress. In the new British restaurants people had to queue at the counter.

Even wartime difficulties did not make me enjoy this method of serving oneself: pick up the tray, slide it along the bars, receive a slop of meat . . . far too much potato and gravy and masses of cabbage…

Mrs Milburn's Diaries:
An Englishwoman's
Day to Day Reflections

Above These women are serving a meal to factory workers in a local hall because their factory canteen has been bombed.

MINCED STEAK

1½ tablespoons (22 ml) **dripping**
2 small onions, finely chopped
1 lb (450 g) minced steak
1 cup stock or water
salt and pepper
1 dessertspoon (12 ml) oatmeal

Melt the dripping in a saucepan. When it is very hot, stir in the onions. Cook for a few seconds, then add the meat. Cook it until it is brown, stirring regularly to prevent it burning. Add the stock or water and some salt and pepper, cover the pan and cook gently for 45 minutes. Add the oatmeal and cook until the oatmeal is ready. Serve with mashed potatoes and green vegetables. Serves 4.

You must ask an adult to help you make this recipe.

Celebrations

It was hard to make special food for a family celebration because so many ingredients were rationed. In 1940, the Ministry of Food banned icing on wedding cakes, because icing used up too much sugar. At a wedding, people might have a small cake with no icing. They hired a big cardboard cake covered in pretend icing to put over the real one.

Left These children are at a street party to celebrate the end of the war in Europe. Everyone had saved up their rations and points so that there would be plenty of food for the celebrations.

EGGLESS CHRISTMAS CAKE

4 oz (100 g) carrot, finely grated
2 tablespoons (30 ml) golden syrup
3 oz (75 g) sugar
4 oz (100 g) margarine
1 teaspoon (5 ml) bicarbonate of soda
½ teaspoon (2.5 ml) almond essence
½ teaspoon (2.5 ml) vanilla essence
4–6 oz (100–150 g) dried fruit
12 oz (300 g) self-raising flour
1 teaspoon (5 ml) ground cinnamon
1 small teacup milk, slightly warmed

Ask an adult to help you cook the grated carrot and syrup over a low heat for a few minutes. Mix together the margarine and sugar until light and fluffy. Stir the bicarbonate of soda into the carrot and syrup mixture, then beat the mixture into the sugar and margarine. Stir in the vanilla and almond essences and the dried fruit. Gently mix in the flour and cinnamon. Mix in the warm milk to make a moist dough. Put the mixture in a greased cake tin, smooth the top and make a deep hole in the centre with a spoon. Bake at 220ºC, gas mark 7, for a few minutes, then turn the oven down to 150ºC, gas mark 2, and bake for 3 hours.

Below Some people went without meat during the week so they could have meat for Sunday lunch.

People saved up their points to buy treats and did the best they could:

Most people had a store cupboard of hoarded tins for the very special occasions: someone's leave, the birth of a baby…

Talking about the War
by Anne Valery

The End of Rationing

The war in Europe ended on 8 May 1945. Food supplies could now be carried across the seas in safety. But in parts of the world where the fighting had taken place, farmland and transport routes had been destroyed. Thousands of farm workers had died. Bad weather ruined many crops. **Rationing** had to continue.

Rations of some foods, such as butter, became smaller than they had been during the war. Bread and potatoes were rationed for the first time.

Above People in London celebrating victory.

Left The war was over, but queuing for food rations went on.

The scramble for food occupies the [most important] place in our lives today . . . prices of vegetables are soaring.

Newspaper report, 1947

People in Britain must have felt that rationing was never going to end. But, little by little, food supplies began to increase. Children were delighted when sweet rationing ended in 1953. In 1954, all rationing came to an end. The battle for food was finally over.

Above These women are protesting against more cuts in the food rations in 1946.

VICTORY SPONGE

1 large raw potato, grated
2 medium raw carrots, grated
1 cup breadcrumbs
1 tablespoon (15 ml) self-raising flour
2 tablespoons (30 ml) sugar
½ teaspoon (2.5 ml) vanilla or lemon essence
1 teaspoon (5 ml) baking powder
3 tablespoons (45 ml) jam

Mix together the grated potato and carrots, breadcrumbs, flour, sugar and vanilla or lemon essence. Stir in the baking powder. Spread the jam around the inside of a warm pudding basin. Put in the pudding mixture, tie on a cover of greaseproof paper, and steam for 2 hours.

Ask an adult to help you steam the sponge.

Glossary

Air-raid shelters Places designed to protect people from bombs during an air raid. Some were big public shelters, others were in people's back gardens.

Armed forces The navy, army and air force.

Blackout The name given to all the things people did to prevent lights showing at night, such as covering windows with thick curtains and not using streetlamps. Lights might have helped enemy bombers to find their targets.

Blancmange A dessert made from milk, similar to a jelly.

Brambles Blackberry bushes.

Campaign Activities that aim to achieve something – for example, the 'Dig for Victory' campaign used posters, rhymes and songs to try to persuade people to grow their own vegetables.

Cod-liver oil Oil taken from the bodies of certain types of fish, including cod, which is high in vitamins.

Dockyard A place where goods are loaded and unloaded from ships.

Dripping The fat that oozes out of meat when it is being roasted or fried. As it cools, it becomes solid, like lard.

Evacuate To move to a place of safety.

Evacuees People who are moved to a place of safety.

Imported Brought into the country.

Knead To squeeze and press with the hands.

Malnutrition Not getting the nutrients the body needs to stay healthy, either through lack of food or not getting the right balance of foods.

Pig swill Waste food that is fed to pigs.

Purée A smooth, thick liquid.

Rationing Making sure that everyone gets an equal share of the goods available.

U-boats German submarines (boats that are designed to travel underwater).

Further Information

Books for young readers
Britain in World War II: Rationing by Alison Cooper
(Hodder Wayland, 2004)
The History Detective Investigates: Rationing by Martin
Parsons (Hodder Wayland, 2000)

Books for experienced readers and teachers
Bombers and Mash: the Domestic Front, 1939–45 by
Raynes Minnis (Virago Press, 1999)
Ration Book Cookery: Recipes and History by Gill
Corbishley (English Heritage, 2004)
*Victory Cookbook: Nostalgic Food and Facts from
1940–1954* by Marguerite Patten (Bounty Books, 2002)
The Wartime Kitchen and Garden by Jennifer Davis
(BBC Books, 1993)
We'll Eat Again: A Collection of Recipes from the War Years
by Marguerite Patten (Hamlyn, 2000)

Websites
http://www.bbc.co.uk/history/ww2children/
Includes a rationing challenge that shows the differences
between wartime diets and those of children today

The website addresses (URLs) included in this book were valid at the
time of going to press. However, because of the nature of the Internet, it
is possible that some addresses may have changed, or sites may have
changed or closed down since publication. While the author and
publisher regret any inconvenience this may cause the readers, no
responsibility for any such changes can be accepted by either the author
or the publisher.

Places to visit
Eden Camp Modern History Theme Museum
Malton
North Yorkshire
YO17 6RT
Telephone: 01653 697777
Fax: 01653 698243
E-mail: admin@edencamp.co.uk

Imperial War Museum London (Headquarters)
Lambeth Road
London SE1 6HZ
Phone: (020) 7416 5320
Fax: (020) 7416 5374
Email: mail@iwm.org.uk

Imperial War Museum North
The Quays
Trafford Wharf
Trafford Park
Manchester M17 1TE
Phone: 0161 836 4000
Fax: 0161 836 4012
Email: iwmnorth@iwm.org.uk

Acknowledgements

Pages 8, 33, 39 *Children of the Blitz* by Robert Westall
(Penguin, 1987)
Page 15 *The Sheltered Days* by Derek Lambert (André
Deutsch, 1965)
Pages 25, 36 *The Wartime Kitchen and Garden* by Jennifer
Davies (BBC, 1993)
Pages 28, 43 *Talking about the War* by Anne Valery (Michael
Joseph, 1991)
Page 29 *Kitchen Front Recipes and Hints* by Ambrose Heath
(1941)
Page 31 *The World is a Wedding* by Bernard Kops (Valentine,
Mitchell and Co, 1973)
Page 41 *Mrs Milburn's Diaries: An Englishwoman's Day to
Day Reflections* (Harrap, 1979)

The recipes
Apple jelly, macaroni and bacon dish, quick vegetable soup,
carrot cookies, cheese pudding, eggless sponge, uncooked
chocolate cake, victory sponge, corned beef hash from *We'll
Eat Again – A Collection of Recipes from the War Years* by
Marguerite Patten (Hamlyn, 1985)
Potato piglets, eggless Christmas cake from *The Wartime
Kitchen and Garden* by Jennifer Davies (BBC, 1993)
Skirly-mirly, minced steak from *Cooking in Wartime* by
Elizabeth Craig (The Literary Press)
Crunchies from *Ration Book Recipes: Some Food Facts
1939–45* by Gill Corbishley (English Heritage, 1990)
Liver savoury from the *Daily Mirror*, 16 August 1940
Marrow pudding, parsnip pudding from the Guernsey
Occupation Museum
Welsh Rarebit from the Ministry of Food leaflet 'How to Use
Stale Crusts'

Index